ON
EVOLUTIONARY
POWER

Also by Julia B. Colwell, PhD

The Inner Map: Navigating Your Emotions to Create the World You Want

The Relationship Ride: A Usable, Unusual, Transformative Guide

The Relationship Skills Workbook: A Do-It-Yourself Guide to a Thriving Relationship

ON EVOLUTIONARY POWER

A Path to Conscious, Sustainable Activism

Julia B. Colwell, PhD

Copyright © 2024 Julia B. Colwell

All rights reserved. No part of this publication may be reproduced, distributed, or transmitted in any form or by any means, including photocopying, recording, or other electronic or mechanical methods, without the prior written permission of the publisher, except for the use of brief quotations in a book review and as permitted by U.S. copyright law.

To request permissions, contact the publisher at info@juliacolwell.com.

ISBN: 978-0-9830506-6-7

Library of Congress Control Number: 2024917671

Front cover design by Tanya Leone
Book design by Tanya Leone
Copyediting by Marj Hahne

Printed in the United States of America

First printing, 2024

Integrity Arts Press
1637 28th Street
Boulder, Colorado 80301

www.JuliaColwell.com
www.EvolutionaryPower.org

for Team Human

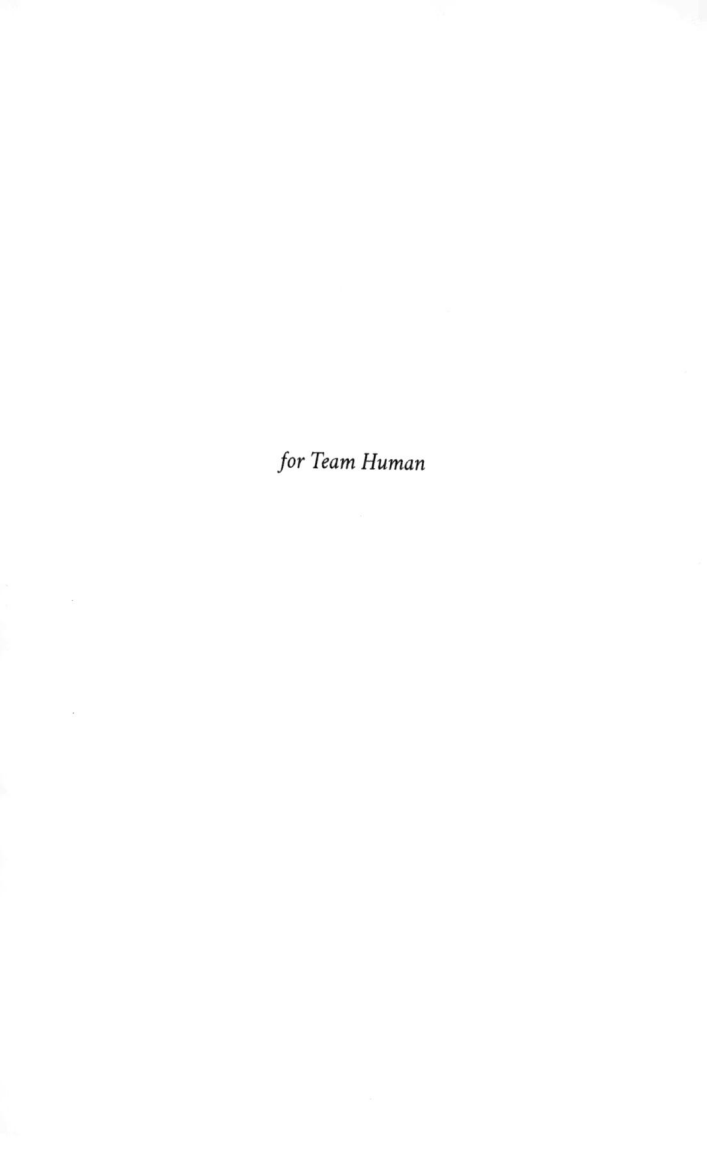

Contents

PROLOGUE:	You are here for this.	**9**
INTRODUCTION:	What is Evolutionary Power?	**13**
STEP 1:	Recognize the signs.	**27**
STEP 2:	Decide to shift.	**33**
STEP 3:	Discover the real issue using SEW.	**37**
STEP 4:	Accept and love what is.	**43**
STEP 5:	Open your focus.	**49**
STEP 6:	Open your heart.	**53**
STEP 7:	Shift to wonder and play.	**57**
STEP 8:	Tell a new story.	**61**
STEP 9:	Commit to Team Human.	**65**
STEP 10:	Choose your next creative action.	**69**
EPILOGUE:	Welcome to *power with*.	**73**

"In this political climate, it is really easy, really easy, to know what we're against, but it is so vital right now for each of us to know what we are for. What we are for is such an expansive, creative, and empowering conversation." [1]

~Andrea Gibson, American poet and activist

---

[1] "White Women: Answer the Call 2024," Answer the Call 2024, July 25, 2024.

Prologue
You are here for this.

Have you ever wondered what you're doing here, why you're here, on Planet Earth, in your body, at this time?

If you have, you're not alone. Our world seems to have gotten crazier, darker. Like there's an unstoppable erosion of values we've held dear: Dignity and respect for all. Equality. Loving each other as we love ourselves. From the perspective of popular culture, humanity is starkly and irrevocably divided, as we've inadvertently relinquished our power, our collective identity, to the autocratic, exploitative, and narcissistic personalities that dominate the central props of our culture: corporate America, the mainstream media, government.

And yet. Beyond all of the noise bombarding us to return to the past, to some "better day," there's a drumbeat, steady, getting louder. It's our collective heart, gathering: in living rooms, over coffee, in blogs and song lyrics, on podcasts and TikTok, at retreat centers and sanghas, on ballfields.

I know you've heard it. It's why you're holding this book. But how can it possibly matter whether you, one person among eight billion, move to this new rhythm?

You've certainly considered, even acted on, your responsibilities. Be informed. Understand the issues. Call your representatives. Get active in campaigns of those you support. Write postcards; knock on doors. Give money. Give more money. And, of course, vote.

With a prayerful nod of appreciation to the leaders and activists in the trenches of our political battles, what if you could do more? What if there were impactful actions you could take every day that were in concert with your personal evolution? That would take you out of the eddy of uncertainty, stress, and worry, and steer you through the rapids of emotional turmoil, back into the stream of life and to the calm of your own center?

Answering the first question for myself, I wrote this book, a creative action possible only because I've been practicing, for thirty years, how to shift my state of being, my sense of my self, my sense of humanity. *I* create my better day. I am *here for this*. I want this agency, this power, for you, too. Let's get evolutionary!

Introduction
What is Evolutionary Power?

This small but mighty book is a guide to a practice that will help you navigate out of the compelling, but limited, vortex of the political moment, and deposit you back into the flow of possibility. Its pages will remind you of the abilities you may have forgotten along the way, or never knew you had. While this practice can't guarantee your preferred outcomes in our government and society, it will release and generate founts of energy—palpable emotional, mental, physical fuel that will reignite your heart, reinspire you to action,

---

2 Modeled after Timothy Snyder's powerful *On Tyranny: Twenty Lessons from the Twentieth Century* (Crown, 2017).

and support you on this wild and exciting ride as a member of this nation, this world, humanity.

As you enter the ideas herein, you're leaving the realm of politics, from the Greek root *politikos*, meaning "of or relating to citizens." You're stepping into what it means to have real power, from the Latin *potere*, "to be able." Because the word "power" has departed from this simple notion, instead long-connoting domination and control, I use the term "Evolutionary Power" to evoke, to remind us, what power truly feels like: that we can *do*—foundationally, as an individual; ultimately, as a collective. We are each the agent in creating the life we want to live, and we can be effective in doing so. We can feel in alignment and flow with what we came to do in this lifetime, and we can experience deep connection with those around us, with all that is, and with ourselves.

In my decades of professional psychotherapeutic practice (and in my own ongoing experience), I've found that the human threat response interrupts and impedes our natural ability to live in this ongoing stream of true power. While most of us understand this mechanism as fight-or-flight (or, more extensively, the five Fs: fight-flight-freeze-faint-fawn), you may not recognize the signals of your own threat response, how it diminishes the quality of your life, and, most important, what do about it.

My intention is that you'll see your own reactivity as the necessary but emotionally ruinous scoundrel it is. While we must have a threat response to survive life in a body—driving a vehicle, fending off a deadly virus, navigating relationships with other reactive humans—it sure can spoil a good time.

On Evolutionary Power: A Path to Conscious, Sustainable Activism turns the axiom "the personal is political" on its head. I'm not the first to propose that the political is personal, but this guide is one of the first to deliver a practical, accessible method for creating—personally, one by one, from the ground up and across and through—a sustainable vision for humanity. Since the first story of creation, power imbalances have existed within most, if not all, relationships—governmental, commercial, familial, intimate, even spiritual. I'm not the first, either, to propose we transform these power imbalances—many of us rally for a shift from *power down* to *power up*—but the premise herein may be your first time encountering the notion of *power with*, that is, Evolutionary Power.

This guide illuminates your individual physiology as a direct *creator* of the path our human species will take. Will you create destructively or constructively? Will you react unconsciously or respond consciously? The ten steps presented in the following chapters will move you out of reactivity, back to your true essence. I recommend you read through them sequentially. Once you've practiced and (somewhat) embodied them, you'll find you can skip around, further practicing the steps that challenge you and employing the steps that restore you most effectively.

Please know that every one of these steps creates a shift in consciousness; you could study and practice any step solely and still benefit. Interfacing with the matters of the external world, whether politics, the media, or a conversation with a friend, you now have an at-the-ready method—one step or the whole sequence—to transform your state anytime you get caught in the vortex of reactivity.

You can unlock your own unlimited potential for creation, knowing that *you* truly matter in our collective human destiny.

Before we get to the steps, I want to introduce you to the context they're based in, that is, the organizing precepts of Evolutionary Power.

We are in control of tapping into what strengthens us—and what weakens us.

Our inner dialogue and external interactions are ongoing sources of real strength or, alternatively, energy drains. As we attune to our body, we can make choices that truly support us.

It can be tempting to rely on short-term bumps of energy that ultimately weaken us. Anger, blame, and self-righteousness are the main culprits in providing those quick hits of adrenaline. Once the initial high wears off, however, we can get the next bump only by finding another reason to be angry, accusatory, self-righteous. What are the long-term effects of this stimulus-reward response? Not only are we immersed in the toxicity of blame, we entangle ourselves with those we're blaming, losing precious vitality.

What actually empowers us? What actually, sustainably, energizes us? Being 100% responsible for the outcomes we're generating: *How am I creating this?* When we wonder this (without self-blame), we reclaim our agency, our freedom to collaborate with life itself to generate *other* possibilities. Rather than focus on how wrong others are, rather than run the fool's errand of trying to change or control them, we're back in the driver's seat of our own existence.

We can be ensnared by the tyranny of our projections and unconscious patterns.

Humans need shortcuts to survive. In every second, we're bombarded by mental and sensory data, so we have to rapidly sort out what matters in order to navigate each next decision, choice, action. Relying on predictions from past experiences means we can function; however, this efficiency leads to all kinds of cognitive biases, stereotyping, and misalignments with our evolving aims and values. We necessarily project how life works from everything we've learned from the past, but are then rather imprisoned by our history. Our culture conditions us such that we can automatically negotiate life and survival needs (the fact that you're alive and awake, reading this, means it did its job), but conditioning is, by definition, unconscious. This survival reliance on automaticity sets us on a course, arguably a static or devolving one, whereby we can easily slip into habitual patterns, believing we're living life.

How do we awaken from unconscious conditioning? We observe when we're in its grasp. We pay attention to the body's reactions to threat and shift it back to our natural state of openness and relaxation. When we return there, beyond our reactivity, we can reengage with life, not through the filter of our stale projections, but consciously, creatively, as it's showing up, no matter how it's showing up.

We create from our state.

Have you ever been in a super-positive frame of mind, rolling along with life, when something happens that disrupts the flow? Have you noticed that your inner narration becomes more negative? And have you noted what typically happens next?

After 50,000-plus hours witnessing people as they traversed the levels of consciousness, from the worst self-hatred, guilt, despair, fear, and anger, to the brightest love, joy, and peace, I know how much power we each have in generating our own reality. In a contracted state, in reactivity, we experience life as compressed, fixed, impossible. In an expansive state, we experience life—and ourselves—as open, resourceful, rich with possibilities.

We create from our state; knowing we can choose our desired state, and knowing how to shift our state (to a more expanded one), is the key to our natural being.

To change your reality (and how it responds to you), change your state.

The late David R. Hawkins, an authority in the field of consciousness research and the developer of the Map of Consciousness®, brilliantly laid out how the levels of consciousness operate at different frequencies. He posited that each frequency sends out an "attractor energy" pulling for a response from the world that mirrors the corresponding level of consciousness. So, when we're in a state of fear, we attune to or attract circumstances that reinforce our fear. When angry, we magnetize reactions that confirm, yes, we should be angry. In other words, once we're operating at a particular level of consciousness, we get plenty of validation that we're right.

I've simplified Hawkins' Map of Consciousness into the Inner Map (see page 23 or download a color version at this link: bit.ly/3zyczgu). As you familiarize yourself with the Inner Map, notice the vertical line extending from Shame up to Peace. Hawkins sorted inner states by frequency, from the most contracted, holding the least energy, to the most expanded and energetically strongest. For example, Shame has the least energy (which is why it's positioned closest to Death); Guilt has more free energy than Shame, Despair more than Guilt, and so on, up through every successive state.

Now locate the horizontal line that separates Reactive Brain from Creative Brain. Though we may think we're somewhat in control of our emotions, every state "Below the Line" is an automatic threat response. When we shift our physiology through successively expanded states up the vertical line, and optimally to a state "Above the Line," life will respond accordingly, partnering with us in cocreating a vortex of positive energy.

Evolutionary Power means aligning with our deepest selves while riding the flow of life.

Hawkins notably differentiated *force* (aka Reactive Brain) from *power* (aka Creative Brain). Force consumes, depletes, takes energy. When we use force, we create a field of resistance, necessarily generating a counterblast of energy from those around us, and from life itself. We can "make things happen," but that requires ongoing effort and energy expenditure as we push and others push back. Force literally exhausts us. Power, on Hawkins' other hand, produces energy as we join with life as it is, revitalizing the conduits of connection within ourselves, with others, and then beyond, with the universe.

Because American culture uses the word "power" to signify domination, control, and, indeed, force, I

What is Evolutionary Power? 23

INNER MAP

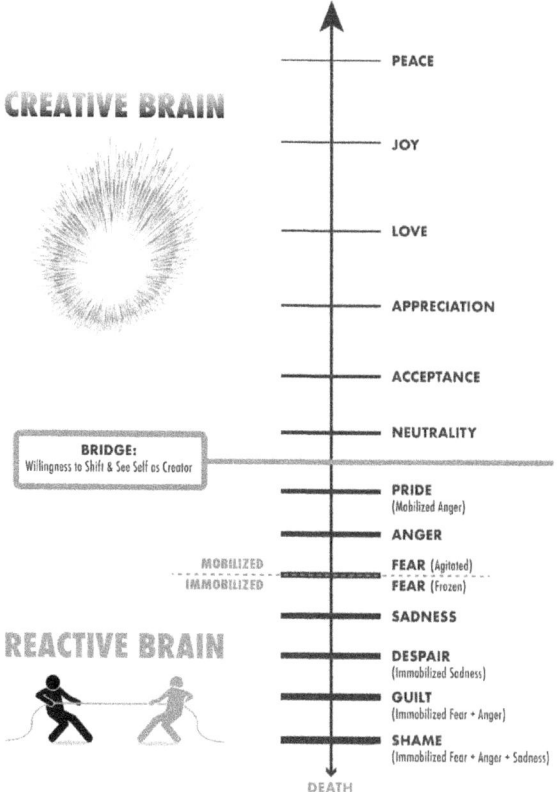

CREATIVE BRAIN

- PEACE
- JOY
- LOVE
- APPRECIATION
- ACCEPTANCE
- NEUTRALITY

BRIDGE: Willingness to Shift & See Self as Creator

- PRIDE (Mobilized Anger)
- ANGER

MOBILIZED
IMMOBILIZED

- FEAR (Agitated)
- FEAR (Frozen)
- SADNESS

REACTIVE BRAIN

- DESPAIR (Immobilized Sadness)
- GUILT (Immobilized Fear + Anger)
- SHAME (Immobilized Fear + Anger + Sadness)

DEATH

For more information see The Inner Map: Navigating Your Emotions to Create The World You Want by Julia Colwell, PhD

© www.JuliaColwell.com, based on "Map of Consciousness" by David Hawkins.
Graphic Design Credit: www.FahneeDesign.com

coined the term "Evolutionary Power" to emphasize the radical reworking of the concept of power as a dynamic of cocreativity, authentic expression, and connection that is directing humanity to evolve to its next level of consciousness.

Evolutionary Power—that is, the zone Above the Line, Creative Brain, *power with*—is generative and replenishing, tapping our optimal cognitive abilities and fine-tuned intuition. When we're in these states of consciousness, we ourselves are the source of our own safety, as we're fully present and able to meet the challenges of life. We're open, resourced, and aligned with our deepest, most essential selves.

Hawkins underscored every individual's impact on humanity's functioning when he enumerated how an expanded state outweighs a large number of people occupying reactive states:

- One person embodying <u>Acceptance</u> counterbalances 90,000 individuals in Reactive Brain.

---

[3] I have roughly translated Hawkins' original numerical structure, from *Power Vs. Force: The Hidden Determinants of Human Behavior* (Turtleback Books, 2002), to my Inner Map.

- One person embodying <u>Appreciation</u> counterbalances 400,000 individuals in Reactive Brain.
- One person embodying <u>Love</u> counterbalances 750,000 individuals in Reactive Brain.
- One person embodying <u>Joy</u> counterbalances 10 million individuals in Reactive Brain.
- One person embodying <u>Peace</u> counterbalances 70 million individuals in Reactive Brain.

One person's level of consciousness—*your* level of consciousness—affects the whole. And the more expanded the state, the larger your impact on your fellow humans, near and far.

On Evolutionary Power outlines ten specific steps you can practice to access, embody, and sustain expanded levels of consciousness. These steps are straightforward, even simple. Still, expect to be challenged: many of us have never learned that we can have any impact on our internal world, let alone how to manage our energy differently.

This is the less-traveled road, so it may seem strange and disorienting. Be your own scientist: experiment with these steps, singly and sequentially, gauging their effects on your state, on your sense of power. And, as with learning any new practice, know that you can commit and recommit. Full embodiment is an ongoing, lifelong endeavor.

I welcome you into this Evolutionary Power movement. Your presence, your consciousness, your creative energy will support humanity in evolving to our next realization of collective potential. Together, we can create a world that celebrates every single one of us, each free to express who we came into this world to be, truly seen and known, and to live from love, joy, dignity, and peace. This is evolutionary activism.

1
Recognize the signs.

Notice the signals from Reactive Brain to step out of old patterns and into new possibilities.

Reactivity is vital to your survival. You detect a threat before you're consciously aware of it and before you can form a thought about it. Your automatic impulse to fight, run, freeze, or go limp allows you to instantly protect yourself in that moment of perceived threat.

When I share the Inner Map, a common response is, "I think I'm in Reactive Brain all the time!" It's startling to realize that the threat response has taken over our lives. Fortunately, most of us shift naturally to Creative Brain when we're sleeping or resting, but American culture sure seems to value a 24/7 stress response, rewarding those who work around the clock, who "do it all," who stoically push through life's obstacles at the expense of their health.

Beyond survival, to simply function in a complicated world, you necessarily rely on an accumulating mass of information based in memories, experiences, perceptions, interpretations, conclusions—all of which shape expectation. Every decision, behavior, interaction extends from predictions calculated, consciously or unconsciously, from what you've learned up until that point. Projections make your life doable.

Can you see how your feelings, thoughts, and actions are rarely created in the here and now?

It's way too easy to escalate a state Below the Line. Your state dictates your thoughts, your thoughts perpetuate your state, and this cycle entrenches your reaction, further strengthened by reality-reinforcing responses from the world that match the attractor energy of your state's frequency.

If you don't know you're in Reactive Brain, you're trapped in a world of threat. Threatened, you deploy one of the five Fs, which short-circuits your awareness of your inner world *and* the external world outside the threat. Your blood flow has been redirected from the thinking brain to instinctive systems built for fighting, fleeing, freezing, fainting, and fawning. Your cognition becomes single-pointed, concrete, rigid, and stereotypical. Since your state continues to direct your thoughts, your solutions are reduced to how you'll fight or get away. If you can't take either action, the freeze response sets in, reducing you to helplessness, or you "disappear" through fainting or fawning.

Reactive Brain—Shame, Guilt, Despair, Sadness, Fear, Anger, Pride—can become so fixed that you think this is just the way the world is. You forget that this isn't your natural state, that this isn't *you*.

But you can wake up, shake yourself out of this unconscious trance. Fortunately, if you pay attention to your body and your mind, you can detect the signals that you've been hijacked by Reactive Brain:

Physiological effects:
- Breath: Rapid, shallow, hard to deepen, from the top of the chest
- Pulse: Rapid, fluttering, difficult to slow
- Muscles: Contracted, agitated, frozen
- Stomach: Tight, nauseated, knotted, queasy
- Chest: Heavy, pained, tight
- Jaw, shoulders, neck: Knotted, tight, painful, clenched
- Whole body: Exhausted, feels sick, feels "bad"

Thoughts:
- "What is wrong with you?"
- "What's going to happen?!"
- "I'm better than they are."
- "They're better than I am."
- "What did I do this time?"
- "I give up."
- "I've lost everything."
- "It's all your fault."
- "I can't figure this out."
- "Want to fight?!"
- "What a jerk!"
- "I don't belong anywhere."
- "It's us against them."
- "I can't count on anyone."
- "This shouldn't be happening."
- (Add yours.) _____
- (Add yours.) _____

Reviewing and extending these lists, identify the signs of your own reactivity right now, in this moment.

2

Decide to shift.

Allow yourself to be with your resistance until your body can move to an authentic YES.

The energy behind your will—to do or not do—is quite the potential resource. Pushing against reality squanders energy; facing into reality allows energetic flow to return. Being willing to move from Below the Line to Above the Line does mean letting go of the known for so much uncertainty, but imagine all the energy you'll accrue, level by level. Imagine all the energy your Creative Brain will have for doing more than surviving, for thriving.

To shift or not to shift—that is the question. As you weigh it, try on these considerations:

Reasons not to shift (provided by my Reactive Brain):

- Other people aren't. They probably know something I don't.
- The known is comfortable.
- It's better to err on the side of survival, so I'd rather trust those signals.
- It's strange, even inhuman, to feel better when so many people are suffering.
- (Add yours.) _____

Reasons to shift (provided by my Creative Brain):

- Flow lives Above the Line. Once I'm in flow, I'm connected to all. Miracles happen there.
- Change is the only constant. Even believing there is a "known" is an illusion.
- Reaction to threat is designed to be brief. Thriving involves moving through the threat response back to a baseline of expansiveness.
- As each of us becomes increasingly expanded, we're directly lifting up the consciousness of all of humanity. Together, we can solve whatever comes our way.
- You can always go back to Reactive Brain if you don't like Creative Brain.
- (Add yours.) _____

I have great appreciation for the human instinct to not be controlled. I've encountered the adult version of "You can't make me!" repeatedly, both personally and professionally. Psychotherapy commonly labels this stubborn proclivity to rebel against another's force "resistance," like it's something to overcome. I believe that this bottom-line unwillingness to be controlled is ground zero of where our true selves are rooted.

I celebrate every person's absolute dedication to their agency.

So, now decide: "Am I willing to shift?" As you entertain this question, let your whole body start with an "absolutely not." Feel the strength of that. That's *you* deciding. Then—wait for it—do you notice a flow of energy that says, "Yes, I am!"?

3

Discover the real issue using SEW.

Bring your awareness to your sensations and emotions, to discover the internal issue masquerading as an external problem.

SEW is a three-step process I've refined over the past thirty years with countless people. SEW drains off the unfelt emotional energy that has kept an issue anchored, and unleashes the aliveness waiting in reserve in the expanded dimensions of Creative Brain. SEW—an acronym evoking "unite"—stands for **S**ensations, **E**motions, **W**ants.

Sensations

The perception of threat disconnects us from our inner awareness as we detect and handle what is wrong. Whether our reaction is mobilized ("Let's fight!" or "Run!") or immobilized ("Oh, no!" or "What should I do?!"), we aren't tracking our internal world.

Your body is trying to get your attention. The only language it has to wave you down are your sensations. Thirst, the urge to urinate, hunger, exhaustion, sexual arousal, a sense of thrill or excitement—these are some of the sensations you may experience throughout the day. If you don't tune in to the body's subtle signals, it will communicate through louder and louder sensations: anxiety, depression, pain, injury, sickness.

Reclaiming yourself from the grip of threat begins with turning your awareness toward your sensations, away from your ongoing stream of thoughts.

Emotions

What we believe to be an emotion is usually a thought masquerading as a feeling. To shift our state, we must pay attention to the energy in motion—*e-motion*—not our brain's expedient label for it.

The states persistently clanging the alarm bells for our survival are Fear, Sadness, and Anger. Reviewing the Inner Map (p. 23), you'll find that all of the other states Below the Line—Shame, Guilt, Despair, and Pride—are actually combinations of Fear, Sadness, and Anger. In threat, the body plays different chords, but they're made of the same three notes.

Fear tells us that we've perceived danger, triggering chemicals that alert our body to run away or, if we can't, to freeze into invisibility. Sadness communicates that we've experienced loss, urging us to cry to signal whomever or whatever we lost to come back. Anger activates us to stop an intrusion or push through an obstacle, whether perceived or actual.

And the pleasurable sensations? The positive emotions? They're waiting for you Above the Line, once your awareness and metabolism clear out the density and stress chemicals of your reactivity. After that, relaxation, a vibrating movement through your limbs, genitals, torso, head, your entire body. And along with that, aliveness, exhilaration, bliss.

Wants

Reactive Brain has countless opinions about what we want. Don't buy into them. They're from the most primitive aspects of self, those that are purely reactive. Wait until you're back home in Creative Brain to even consider what you want. Because Creative Brain goes big. Because Creative Brain interfaces with your most essential self, with the people around you, and with expanded realities invisible to human perception. With this in mind, we'll revisit the "W" step in Step 10.

Your task right now is to tune in to your sensations to accurately identify which reactive emotions they are conveying:

- Fear: Contracted muscles, knotted stomach, queasiness, shakiness, immobility, shallow breath, rapid pulse
- Sadness: Heaviness in the heart, lump in the throat, slumped posture
- Anger: Burning energy up through the torso and into the head, clenched fists/jaw, headache, sore neck/shoulders/lower back

Now, let your attention wander through your whole body. What sensations are "loudest"? Focusing on these, one by one, which emotion can you trace them to: Fear? Sadness? Anger?

This sorting is the communication link between your body and your mind. As you put all of these pieces together, you'll expediently uncover the real issue. It's not out there; it's not about anyone or anything else. It's you telling you that you've perceived a threat, a loss, an intrusion or obstacle. Once you've received the body's message, breathe into each sensation and emotion until you notice your body shift, even just a little bit.

You have a truly incredible ability to move your negative inner experiences through your body by focusing your awareness on your sensations and emotions, and shifting to Creative Brain. Instead of trying to control and solve some problem your Reactive Brain has located in the external world, you're now squarely in charge of changing YOU. This is where your real power—evolutionary power—lives.

4

Accept and love what is.

*Accept and love what is to move you
out of resistance and into the expanded
territory of Creative Brain and flow.*

Fear, Sadness, and Anger (and the other states existing Below the Line) are all adaptive responses to toting a body around in a three-dimensional world. Fear charges you up to handle an oncoming car or an irate boss. Sadness draws your body in for protection as you adjust to life without someone or something you've lost. Anger generates the oomph to create a boundary against perceived intrusions, or the vim to persist in the face of obstacles.[4]

Reactive Brain emotions are signs of resisting life, wanting it to be different from how it's showing up. No matter your desires, no matter your opinions about what's happening, one thing you can absolutely count on: reality will do what it wants, regardless.

Referring back to the Inner Map (p. 23), note what's directly Above the Line: Neutrality and Acceptance. Neutrality says, "It is what it is." Acceptance goes further: "I accept life as it is, right

---

[4] For a complete explanation of the adaptive function of every level of consciousness, see my book *The Inner Map: Navigating Your Emotions to Create the World You Want* (Integrity Arts Press, 2020).

here, right now." Just like you accept what month, day, or year it is.

Is such clarity possible if you're caught in the throes of Reactive Brain, mad that this is happening, sad that that happened, afraid about what will happen? You absolutely get to feel anger, grief, fear. This is how you know you're experiencing life. But your whole world will darken while you're in their thrall. Move through them, and you've returned to facing life directly, as it is.

You don't have to like what is happening to accept it. Acceptance doesn't put a stamp of approval on whatever is going on. It does, however, move you through the contraction of anger, sadness, fear, and spin you out of all that energy you're wasting in force, pushing against others as they push back.

I accept life as it is, right here, right now.

Notice how that feels in your body, the receding of tension, the settling into the moment.

Welcome to the realm of Creative Brain.

Let's supercharge this experience by adding the regenerative power of Love:

I love all of what is, as it is.

If your Reactive Brain is protesting, "How in the world can I love all that's wrong in the world?!" give it some reassurance. You're not loving what is for any reason. You're loving it because, well, you're choosing to.

Now, identify a circumstance of your life that you think "should not be happening." Say deliberately, until you feel your body open, "I accept this as it is."

Now think of someone or something you love *easily*. Take a moment to really consider who or what that is. Feel sensations of love surging through your body. Enjoy the warmth, the expansiveness. Now imagine "reality," whatever that means to you.

And, lastly, the big move? Wrap reality with this warm, wonderful blanket of love.

Just because.

---

5   This exercise appears in Gay Hendricks' book *Learning to Love Yourself* (CreateSpace, 2011).

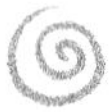

5

Open your focus.

*Open your visual field to change your
brain waves and your higher vision.*

One of the most powerful practices I use to change my physiology is Dr. Les Fehmi's Open Focus technique. Fehmi's research on biofeedback led him to a rather startling discovery: we can change our brain waves through shifts in our visual field.

Contemporary Western culture places a premium on what Fehmi calls "narrow-objective focus." Spending most of your days focused and alert causes the brain to generate beta waves—a state associated with the stress response. The payoff in concentration—at work meeting deadlines, at home watching children, on the street rushing to appointments—comes with an enormous cost: the body, marinating in cortisol and adrenaline, is exhausted of its physical and emotional resources and hence is blocked from its natural rejuvenation process.

Fehmi found that "open focus" generates alpha brain waves, a state of calm alertness—what meditation practices are designed to do—and links

---

6   Les Fehmi, PhD, and Jim Robbins, *The Open-Focus Brain: Harnessing the Power of Attention to Heal Mind and Body* (Trumpeter, 2007).

it to increased creativity and decreased anxiety and depression.

Open focus enhances Creative Brain.

You can open your focus in a variety of ways. Here's the one I rely on (especially when my thoughts seem stuck on what's wrong): Without moving your eyes or head, focus on a point in front of you. Now expand your peripheral vision, noticing more and more of what appears to each side of you, until you can perceive what is outside your visual field. Let your vision blur a bit, and breathe.

Notice your body. Do you feel more open and relaxed? Are you in Creative Brain?

6

Open your heart.

Open your heart to further expand and sustain your level of consciousness.

Centuries of sages have extolled and glorified, and schooled their disciples in, accessing the heart's vast, transformative energy. Let's plug you into this powerhouse.

Echoing Michael Singer, if you want an open heart, don't close it!

This requires you to drop into your awareness of your body, especially the area surrounding your heart. Breathe into this space. Does it resonate with your breath, and relax and open? Or does it feel blocked, stopping any flow?

Reactive Brain says it's a bad idea to have an open heart. The world is dangerous, right? You don't want to get hurt. Better to stay closed, shut off. Safe.

Don't believe your Reactive Brain. Access the biggest energy source you have by opening the portal to love.

---

7 Michael A. Singer, *The Untethered Soul: The Journey Beyond Yourself* (New Harbinger Publications/Noetic Books, 2007).

Let's try it again. Focus on your chest. Place your hand on your heart. Inhale. Exhale. Relax. Tell yourself the narrative that arises naturally from Creative Brain: Accept life as it is. Even love it. Just as it is.

Let your breath expand your whole heart, feeling it bloom, allowing life to enter as it is.

7

Shift to wonder and play.

Wonder and play transport you out of the known and into cocreation with life.

Reactive Brain prefers the known. It wants to be able to protect you by predicting danger based on past experiences. The known masquerades as certainty—no gray area, no doubt, no questioning, no not-knowing. How do you free yourself from Reactive Brain's uncompromising perception of humanity as wrong, dangerous, destructive to all of life?

You have to give up the need to be right. You have to not think you know. You have to be willing to be wrong, to not know, to open to learn.

Not being right, not knowing—what does it get you? Well, new possibilities. New thoughts outside the confines of Reactive Brain. New solutions previously unimagined. Interfaces with untapped potential. And, ultimately, dreams and visions fulfilled—of your life, of the world—that once seemed impossible.

Say this aloud: "I wonder…" Do you like how that rolls in your mouth?

Now, open to wonder, let your curiosity get piqued.

Are you feeling the tickle of exhilaration? That's where wonder takes me. And it prepares me for my favorite experience of all: play.

When you enter the realm of play, you're in the moment, at the ready. Your playmate Life tosses you an experience—random, new, same ol' same ol'— and waits to see what you toss back.

Imagine the following scenarios and these possible play-full responses to them:

Flat tire?

- Admire the roadside.
- Interact with the tow-truck driver.
- (Add yours.) _____

Cancer?

- Receive the care and kindness of doctors, nurses, and support-group survivors.
- Experience the miracles of what millions of human hours of research have yielded.
- (Add yours.) _____

Friend in Reactive Brain?

- Hold their hand.
- Put on some music and invite them to dance with you.
- (Add yours.) _____

Play moves you beyond your controlled existence, expressing your most expanded self as you cocreate with your teammates in this game of life.

Now, identify something you've enjoyed being right about. Say, until you feel your body open, "I wonder… is there a new way for me to see this?"

Now consider an experience that you've deemed to be negative or wrong. In the moment of that experience, how might you have played with what life brought you?

8

Tell a new story.

Craft your inner narration and outer words from Creative Brain.

Humans have always told stories. Stories are how we organize experience.

Tune in to your thoughts right now. What are you saying in the background thrum of your mind? That it's a good idea to keep reading? A not-so-good idea? That you can do this? That you can't? That you'd rather be outside? That the world is a dangerous/friendly/horrifying/glorious place? That the future is scary/wonderful/apocalyptic?

When we're overwhelmed by the stimuli the brain is inputting from our senses, we have no time or resources to perceive it objectively. To survive from moment to moment, we end up sorting life through our patterns, biases, and preconceptions, creating a narrative, however unconstructive, that allows us to keep going.

Storytelling hypnotizes us into levels of consciousness. The lyrics of a song, a TV drama, the family myths, a news article, a partner's work complaint, a friend's gossip—stories, and the states they anchor us to, live in every sentence, and even in one word, uttered.

If you watch what you say to yourself, you can figure out where you are on the Inner Map. Repeating the story—each time getting more emphatic, embellishing it with keener details—entrenches you in its attendant state.

So many stories—personal, familial, cultural, and especially political—anchor us to Reactive Brain:

- "I can't believe those people are so ignorant!" Anger. Pride.
- "Oh, no! This can't be!" Fear.
- "The world is in terrible trouble." Sadness. Fear.
- "We're beyond the point of being able to save ourselves." Despair.
- "It's my fault." Shame. Guilt.
- (Add yours.) _____

It's not useful to dispute any of these stories. When you're in Reactive Brain, such stories are true. But such stories don't connect you to your real, evolutionary power. *That* exists in Creative Brain. It's time, then, to thwart Reactive Brain's hijacking of your storytelling by telling stories that anchor you to the states Above the Line:

- "Life is happening." Neutrality. Acceptance. Peace.
- "I accept and love life as it is." Acceptance. Love.
- "I appreciate the world, and all of its beings, as it is right now." Acceptance. Appreciation.
- "Joy is available here and now, in this moment." Joy.
- "Nature is perfect. We are nature." Love. Peace.
- "All is well." Acceptance. Peace.
- (Add yours.) _____

If you're going to narrate a story—and you will as long as your mind is alive—write one that enlivens you. Tell it and retell it so that it becomes your felt experience, your evolutionary power.

Now, consider a negative story you've been telling yourself. Locate its attendant state on the Inner Map (p. 23). Choose a state in Creative Brain, and retell the story from that level of consciousness.

9
Commit to Team Human.

Join the eight billion of us, supporting each other to uniquely contribute our essence toward evolutionary progress.

Try out this thought: *All humans are my equal.* What sensations, emotions, and thoughts arise?

As much as we aspire to the ideal of equality, our actions, behaviors, thoughts, and utterances infrequently align with it. We're so used to hierarchy. We've been vying for gold stars and blue ribbons since kindergarten. Our media ranks the 10-best-this, the 5-worst-that. We habitually compare ourselves with everyone else, even with our past and future selves.

Of course, comparison and competition are fundamental Reactive Brain. When we perceive threat, we automatically experience a power differential: if we see ourselves as bigger, stronger, faster, we get mobilized (fight); if weaker, less than, not good enough, we get immobilized (flight, freeze, faint, fawn).

Fundamental Creative Brain is collaboration. We cocreate as playmates, on the same side. All of us. Each and every one of us. We celebrate our differences because differences make a complete, well-rounded team.

Are you willing to leap into the expanded unknown, to the highest vision? Here it is again:

I commit to seeing my fellow humans as my equals, allies, and teammates.

Identify someone you're on the same team with—a friend, a sibling, a spouse, a playmate in an extracurricular activity. Breathe into your feeling of affinity with them. Now extend that feeling to someone a bit more challenging, perhaps a colleague. As you are able to bring them in, continue to expand your team more and more broadly, until you can encircle the world.

10

Choose your next creative action.

Execute an action from Above the Line, allowing your most expanded self to contribute to the world.

You've done it. You've noticed, chosen to shift, felt into your body, uncovered the real issue, accepted and loved what is, opened your focus and your heart, wondered, played, and told a new story. You even signed up to be on Team Human's roster.

Wow. Do you feel plugged into new sources of power and potential?

When you learned about SEW, I cautioned you to wait until you're reliably in Creative Brain to envision what you really want. Just as with Reactive Brain (pp. 30–31), if you pay attention to your body and your mind, you can detect the signals that you're residing in Creative Brain:

Physiological effects:
- Breath: Deep and long
- Pulse: Slow and regulated
- Muscles: Relaxed, fluid
- Stomach: Relaxed
- Chest: Open
- Jaw, shoulders, neck: Relaxed
- Whole body: Relaxed, engaged, fluid

Thoughts:
- "How can I support them?"
- "Life is good!"
- "I feel connected with everything and everyone."
- "So much is possible!"
- "Tell me more."
- "I know what to do."
- "What's right about this?"
- "I feel safe."
- "All is well."
- "I can do this."
- "We're in this together."
- "I'm part of this."
- "How can I serve?"
- (Add yours.) _____
- (Add yours.) _____

If you're not in Creative Brain right now, revisit the first two steps of the SEW process (pp. 38–42) to metabolize Reactive Brain's sensations and emotions.

If you are in Creative Brain, breathe into your open heart and tune in to how experiencing your world from Creative Brain has altered your current sense of life and reality.

Now it's time to ask, "What do I *really* want? For myself? For Team Human?" Drop into your body and listen. Write down what you hear.

Now ask, "What action can I take that's aligned with what I want?" Again, drop into your body, listen, and write down what you hear. Record a "by when" timeframe. Commit to following through.

Indeed, even the most simple and easeful action that comes from Creative Brain, your essential self, is the perfect action. And any action you execute at a level of consciousness Above the Line benefits not only yourself but your family, your friends, your colleagues, your communities, your entire human team.

Epilogue
Welcome to *power with*.

Let's step back and fully appreciate humanity's ability to survive over millennia. Our proliferation to a global population of eight billion humans attests to how well the unconscious processes of reactivity and projection have served us. However, what got us here could be exactly what leads to our species' demise.

Fortunately, the march toward Reactive Brain's ultimately destructive outcomes is being met by a groundswell of information, teachings, and commitments to becoming conscious. I believe that each one of us is here for this very reason: to be a bridge from our old reactive patterns to previously unimagined possibilities.

As you try out, practice, and embody the ten steps that *On Evolutionary Power* offers, know that you are reclaiming your true power as a human, far beyond the soup of *power up* and *power down* that we've all been simmering in. You are my teammate; I am yours. Together, with Team Human, we get to play in the wondrous realm of *power with*. We must bring together all of our unique talents so that humanity—and all beings—can collectively thrive.

I'll see you out there on the field.

About the Author

JULIA B. COLWELL, PHD, is the founder and director of the Evolutionary Power Institute, in Boulder, Colorado. She conducts research, trains practitioners, and teaches laypeople in the practices of Evolutionary Power. She is the author of *The Relationship Ride: A Usable, Unusual, Transformative Guide*, *The Relationship Skills Workbook: A Do-It-Yourself Guide to a Thriving Relationship*, and *The Inner Map: Navigating Your Emotions to Create the World You Want*.

Photo: Cynthia Hildner

www.JuliaColwell.com
www.EvolutionaryPower.org

Printed in the USA
CPSIA information can be obtained
at www.ICGtesting.com
JSHW072108180924
69823JS00007B/27

9 780983 050667